AF426611

Como SQUID*

Mejores decisiones, menos remordimientos

*****
Detente
Pregunta
Entiende
Imagina
Decide

To you and your loved ones
from the SQUIDminders

including Drs. Mel, ZaSm & Zimbardo

For updates on this book
Visit us @
www.squidminders.org
version
22Aug22

Ready to learn How to SQUID?

We're SQUIDminders. We SQUID our minds and mind our squid. We're here to help you understand how your brain works and how to make better decisions by learning how to SQUID as often as possible.

Stop... ask Questions... Understand... Imagine your choices, then Decide what to do.

Let's get started!

Created by: The SQUIDminders – @squidminders
Illustrated by: Stacey Quigley – @quigley_living and
Laboogie – @laboogieart
Adaptaciones por Alejandra Levy y el equipo SQUIDminders
Edited by: William de Melo and Brandy Thomas

a QoLx © Publication

HOW TO SQUID

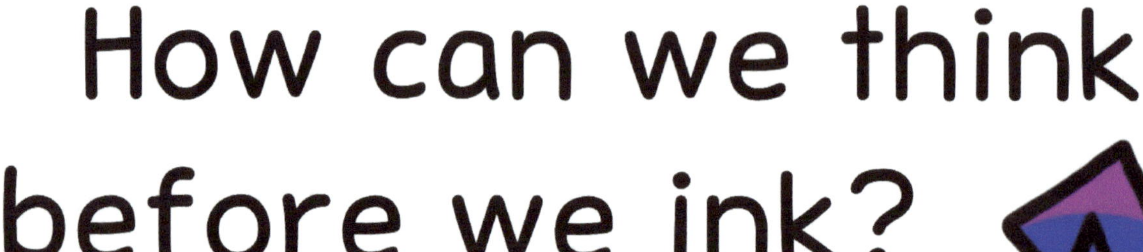

How can we think before we ink?

Whenever you feel like something is wrong, can you

STOP to ask

QUESTIONS to better

UNDERSTAND? Can you

IMAGINE your choices, then

DECIDE on a plan?

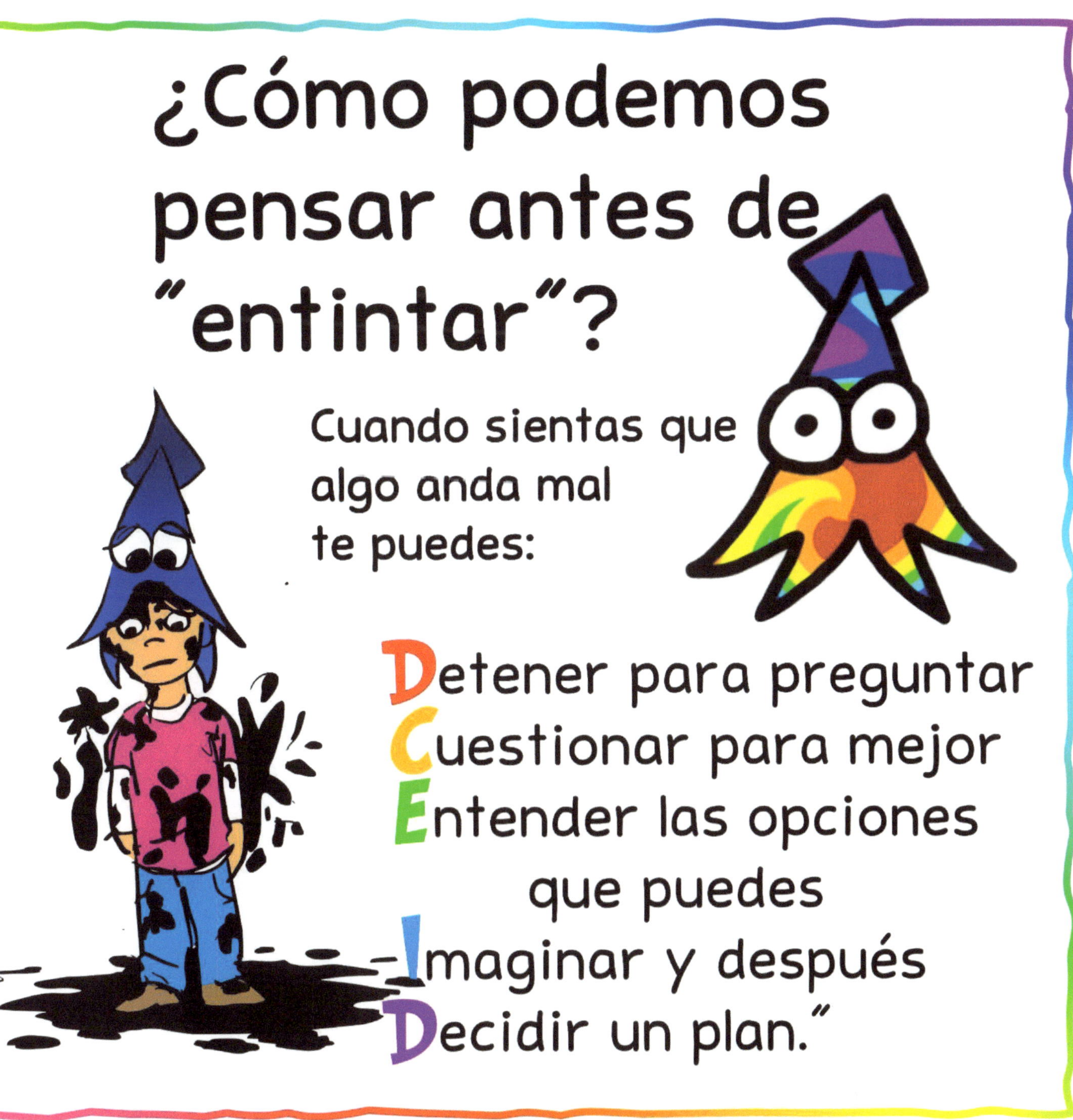

¿Cómo podemos pensar antes de "entintar"?

Cuando sientas que algo anda mal te puedes:

Detener para preguntar
Cuestionar para mejor
Entender las opciones que puedes
Imaginar y después
Decidir un plan."

You and Your SQUID Brain:
Can You Think Before You Ink?

by Dr Mel & the SQUIDminders

You might be surprised
to learn what we did,
but now we can show you
your very own **squid**!

It's like part of your **BRAIN**
that is hidden from view,
but it often drives
what you say and you do.

Tú y tu *SQUID* cerebro:
¿Puedes pensar antes de entintar?

por Dr. Mel & los SQUIDminders

Te sorprenderá
aprender lo que yo hice,
Ahora te enseño como
tu propio *squid* mentalices.

Es la parte de tu CEREBRO
que escondida está.
A menudo lo que dices y
haces el *squid* orquesta.

Whenever your **squid** FEELS
like something is wrong,
it's right there to tell you,
it doesn't take long.

It turns different
COLORS
and can make
your heart race.

It can make you get LOUDER
or scrunch up your face!

Siempre que se **SIENTE**
que algo anda mal,
Ahí para decírtelo el
squid es el central.

Se transforma
en diferentes
COLORES
y hace que
tu corazón
se acelere.

Puede hacer que tu cara se
ARRUGUE y tu voz se eleve.

Your **squid**, it turns out,
will squirt **INK** in distress.
If it feels overwhelmed,
you can make quite a **MESS!**

So what can
you do when your
squid starts
to yelp?

You can
ask some
good questions
if you want to
HELP!

¡Al parecer tu *squid*
en peligro está,
TINTA expulsará y
un grar **LIO** provocará!

Entonces,
¿qué puedes hacer
cuando tu *squid*
se abruma?

Si quieres **AYUDARLE**
buenas preguntas
debes hacer,
he aquí algunas:

Could you try to distract
it before it REACTS?

Could you cover
your mouth
before it
ATTACKS?

Could you take a deep
BREATH,

count to TEN,
WALK AWAY?

Then ask your **squid**
What it most needs to say?

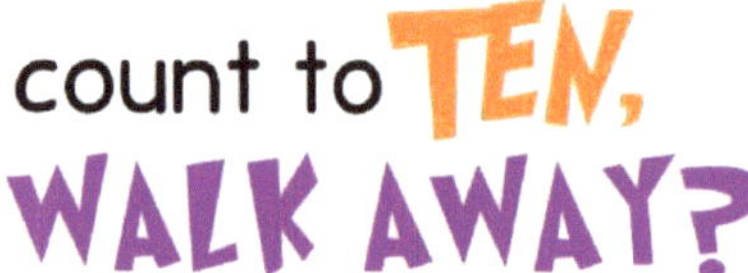

¿Puedes distraerlo antes de que **REACCIONE?**

¿Puedes cubrir tu boca antes de que **ATAQUE?**

¿Podrías **RESPIRAR** hondo,

contar hasta **DIEZ?**
¿ALEJARTE?

Preguntarle a tu *squid* te explique sus necesidades.

Where can you go if you just need to hide?

How can you help your **squid** cool off **INSIDE?**

Could you **STOP** to ask **QUESTIONS** to better **UNDERSTAND?** Could you **IMAGINE** your choices then **DECIDE** on a plan?

¿A dónde te puedes ir si quieres huir?

DETENTE un momento para que mejores **PREGUNTAS** puedas hacer y así a tu *squid* puedas **COMPRENDER**. **IMAGINA** tus opciones y **DECIDE** un plan.

Before you return from where ever
you go, make a plan to come back,
and try to talk
S L O W...

Things might get messy if
your feelings still hurt,
but maybe good questions can
stop a **squid**
SQUIRT!

Now I have a question
that I must ask you!
If there's a **squid** in
your BRAIN,
do I have one, too?

Regresa de donde estás, habla
L E N T O...
evitarás un volcán.

Si tus sentimientos aún
están heridos, las cosas en
caos se pueden volver.

Buenas preguntas evitan que tu
squid **ARROJE TINTA**
y eche todo a perder.

Te voy a hacer una
pregunta más:
¿Si en tu **CEREBRO**
un *squid* hay,
crees que en el mío
alguno hay?

Why and How to S.Q.U.I.D. our Squid Minds:
Stop - Question - Understand - Imagine - Decide

"This is Dr. Philip Zimbardo. It's 2022, a strange time to be alive.
For all the good humans can do, humanity is in trouble."

Suffering surrounds us, and we can feel helpless to do anything about it.
We each need to learn how to SQUID. SQUID is five steps to trigger mindfulness
when we need it most, especially whenever you feel something isn't right.

Better choices mean fewer regrets, and better lives!

You might not think you need this book, but you know other people who do,
urgently. Each of us, including you, can be an everyday hero, every day,
using SQUID to help us save humanity from ourselves.

Why, When & How to SQUID?
Whenever we feel like something is wrong,
Where do we feel it first?
Do our hearts race, our faces flush?
Where do we feel it worst?

Whenever we feel like something is wrong, can we:

Stop to ask

Questions to better

Understand? Can we

Imagine our choices? Then

Decide on a plan?

WHY should we learn how to SQUID?

- Change a habit that isn't useful
- Decrease the times we react on autopilot
- Make better choices
- Understand our options
- Have fewer regrets
- Increase quality of life (QoL) for ourselves and those around us
- Help the world become a better place

Although our human brains are capable of analysis and imagining options, how often do we do that?

When we ignore the possible consequences, what does that cost us?

WHEN should we SQUID?

Before our thinking brain is able to take in what's what, our emotional toad brains are reacting: Fight, Flight, Freeze or Fawn. Our bodies give us signals like yellow lights. Do we run the red? Or interrupt our autopilot to SQUID?

- Whenever we want to consider our choices
- When something feels wrong
- When we witness something wrong

HOW can we learn to SQUID?

We can train our emotional minds. Before a messy squirting ink situation arises, we can examine and understand our individual squid minds.

Step 1: Get to know your squid by reflecting on the past:

Imagine your squid mind is a character you can see and talk with.

★ How does your squid ink when it is upset? We are "inking" when we say or do hurtful things to ourselves or others. Do you yell at other people?
Do you say mean things to yourself?

★ Where in your body does the upset squid first show up?
Does your heart beat faster? Does your
face feel hotter? Do you clench your fists or jaw? Does your throat feel tight, or your stomach ache? What do you notice first?

★ What type of messes does your squid make that you want to avoid?

Step 2: Plan for ways you might reduce your squid's inky messes in the future:

★ What kinds of things trigger or annoy you and upset your squid?

★ Think creatively about how you could respond in a less messy way next time.

★ What does "Think Before You Ink!" mean to you?

Is there something you can have with you to remind your squid?

Step 3: If your squid isn't ready for questions:

★ "Give a gift to your future self" by packing an "Emotional Emergency Kit"
(an EEK bag). Good distractions can be one of the best ways to help calm your squid.

★ Pack your EEK bag with different things you love, with things that could distract and calm your squid mind.

★ Puzzles, games or books, anything packable that help you change focus.

Step 4: Select escape havens ahead of time, places you can go if your squid begins to be upset:

★ Do this at home as well as places you may visit.

★ The escape haven should allow you to be alone and unobserved or heard.

★ A bathroom might be one of the best escape options. When you are in there, you can check in with your squid, even talking to yourself in the mirror if that helps.

Step 5: Mind your squid during your days and nights:

★ You can care for your squid like a pet and get it what it needs: food, water, sleep and love.

★ When you wake up, check on your squids type of emotion, and look for ways to begin the day without squid upset.

★ During the day use S.Q.U.I.D. (as described next).

★ Check in with your squid at night before you go to sleep. Help it get a good nights rest so you can start your next day fresh.

★ Squid brains do much better when they've slept well.

HOW do we SQUID? (Think Before You Ink!)

Step 1: We try to Stop when we are aware of our squid signals!

The most important step is being able to notice when our -- is on autopilot or starting to get upset. The faster we notice the signs of trouble, the faster we might be able to help. If we don't help refocus our squids quickly, we might be unable to prevent them from inking.

Step 2: We try to Question our squids

Any question might help, but the best questions will be the ones that give our squids a chance to calm down. Could we ask our squid. "Do you need a distraction?" Or "Why do I feel like something is wrong?" If we are trying to help someone else, we try to choose questions carefully to help their squid calm down instead of either of us getting more upset.

Step 3: We try to Understand the bigger picture

By taking even a moment to look at the bigger picture of what is going on, we can make a better decision about what to do next. We try to look for more than one perspective about what is going on and why. To improve our understanding, we ask ourselves more questions. Examples: Am I overreacting?" "Have I had enough sleep, food, water?" "What's going on for the other people involved?"

Step 4: We try to Imagine the possibilities

One of the reasons we ink without thinking is that we aren't imagining what is likely to happen next. We try to imagine how other people are likely to respond to different things we could say or do. We also try to imagine some options for what we want to see happen and what we could try to help get there.

 Then we **Decide** what we want to try next

Even if we decide to do just what we were going to do on autopilot, at least we still practiced questioning ourselves before we did it. The habit of questioning ourselves more frequently gives us many more opportunities to make better decisions.

Sometimes we still make mistakes, but we keep trying! Life gets better!

Join our team at QoL-x

What is the foundation for our Quality of LIfe? The stuff going on between our ears and throughout our bodies and minds. Where can we learn about this? Not usually in school. Kids nowadays know more about Tyrannosaurus rex than about their own neocortex.

Our goal at Quality of Life eXperiments (QoL-X.org) is to help people of all ages develop metacognition and mindfulness. A huge number of humans, with our squid minds, to what is here. We need more people like you. Find us at QoL-X.org (or email us at squidminders@gmail.com) to learn what we're working on as well as what we have for you and your favorite humans. We invite you to join our creative thinking for this quality-of-life-changing work!

SQUID and Our
Creatures of Habit

INNER VOICES

There are choirs of creatures inside my mind.
Once I knew where to look they weren't hard to find.

My Creatures of Habit are my inner voices.
They frame my perceptions and drive all my choices.

My imaginary friends, some kind and some mean.
Live in my squid brain, to you and others, unseen.

My squid brain controls what I do and I say.
It drives all my choices throughout every day.

It pulses with color, swims through life, and can squirt.
Especially when I feel scared, angry or hurt.

My Bird Brains might notice when something seems wrong.
They fly in to look closely, and ask questions in song.

They are my sensory sentries, paying attention to things,
A sudden sight of red, the loud flap of wings.

My Pachyderm Brains label what my senses perceive.
My Hippo on campus can be quick to retrieve

The memories that my elephant won't let me forget
Especially the times Ive been filled with regret.

My toad brains most often will croak and complain.
They're my emotional systems, my joys and my pain.

Whenever they feel like something is wrong,
They flood me with chemistry, it doesn't take long.

My QoL Cats live in my neocortex, behind my forehead.
They've been with me since birth and will stay 'til I am dead

They strive to be good, with positive thoughts
They can see my big goals and help connect dots.

Mean Cats live there, too, hiss their thoughts in my ears.
Dark voices, making choices, deeply based on my fears.

Whenever notice they're getting too loud,
My brain feels foggy, all covered in cloud.

Those clouds turn out to be a constant chemical wash
The choices we make then can turn dreams into squash.

My atom ants are the messengers who pass info along
Hormones and neurotransmitters are the notes in our song.

When I look in the mirror and imagine all this inside me,
It can seem overwhelming, but it helps me to see.

All the noise between my ears, all the joys, all the tears
My creatures are with me across all of my years.

Which Creatures of Habit are in Your Head?

The Creatures of Habit Wheel of Wisdom
Las Criaturas del Habito Rueda de la Sabiiduria

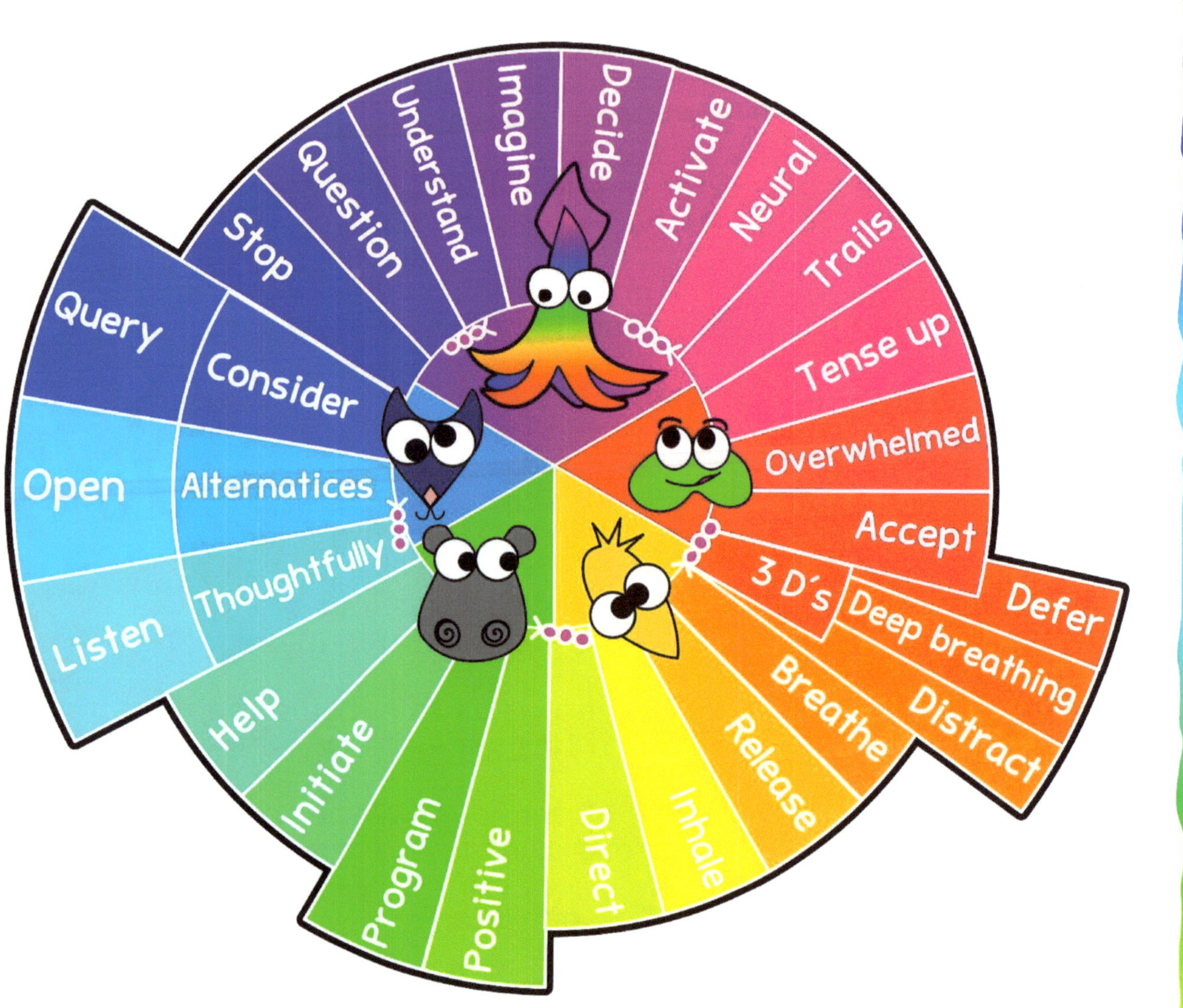

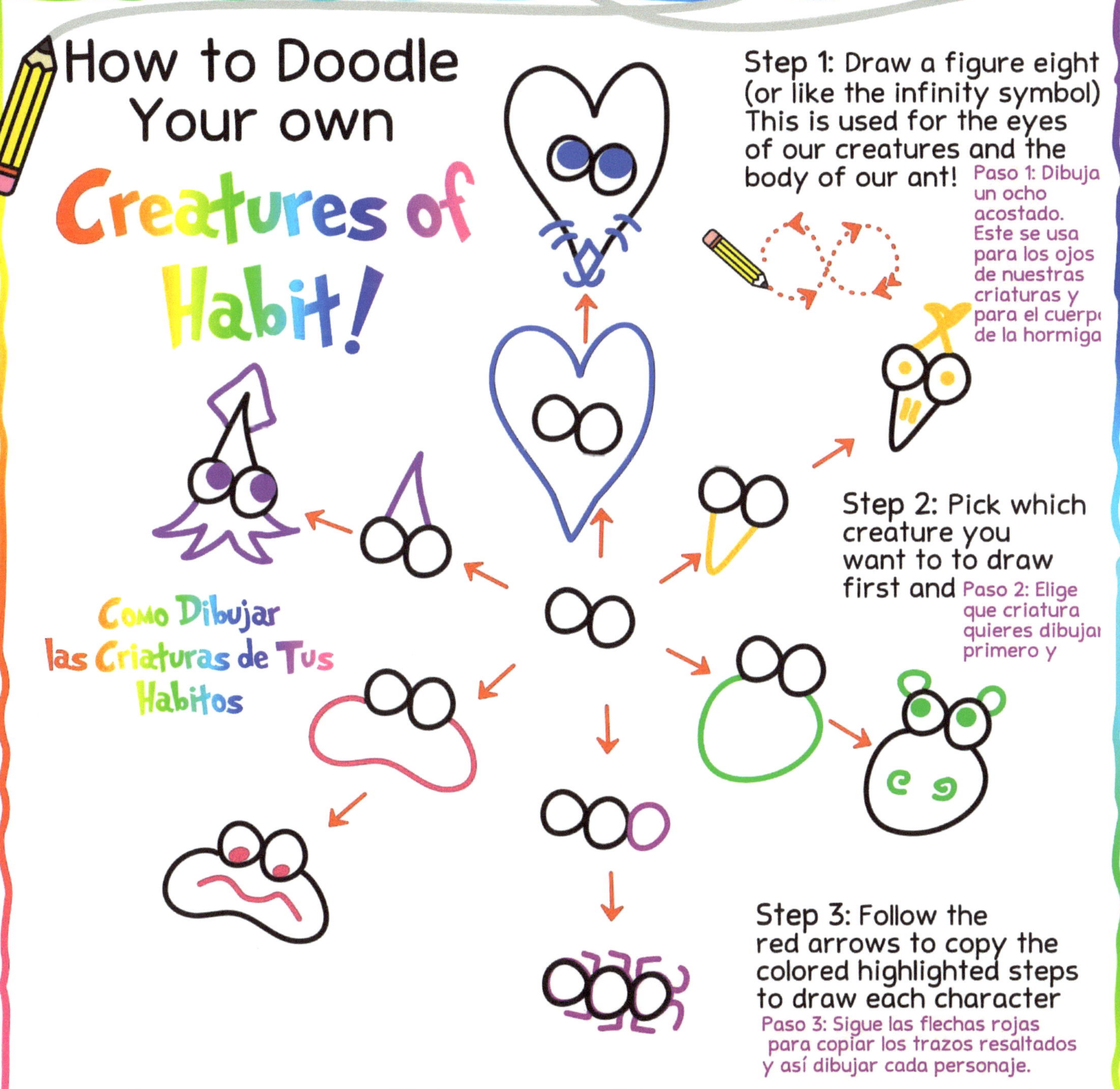

How to Doodle Your own Creatures of Habit!

Como Dibujar las Criaturas de Tus Habitos

Step 1: Draw a figure eight (or like the infinity symbol) This is used for the eyes of our creatures and the body of our ant!

Paso 1: Dibuja un ocho acostado. Este se usa para los ojos de nuestras criaturas y para el cuerpo de la hormiga

Step 2: Pick which creature you want to to draw first and

Paso 2: Elige que criatura quieres dibujar primero y

Step 3: Follow the red arrows to copy the colored highlighted steps to draw each character

Paso 3: Sigue las flechas rojas para copiar los trazos resaltados y así dibujar cada personaje.

BIRD

and the CREATURES of habit

in BRAILLE

Breathe
Inhale
Relax
Direct your attention back to your breathing.

The Glyphs for Bird

Bird doodles you can try when you need a moment to make sure you ask the right questions.

- In hyper focused creative problem solving = Crow

- Natural State of mind = Hummingbird

- The sentry

HIPPO

and the CREATURES of habit

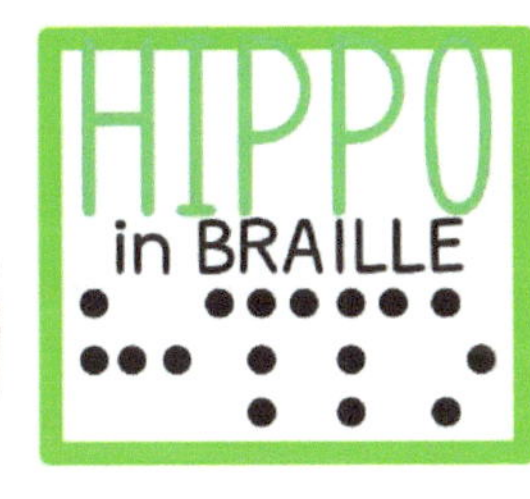

The Glyphs for Hippo

an easy doodle for remembering why we got so upset and to understand why we did in the first place.

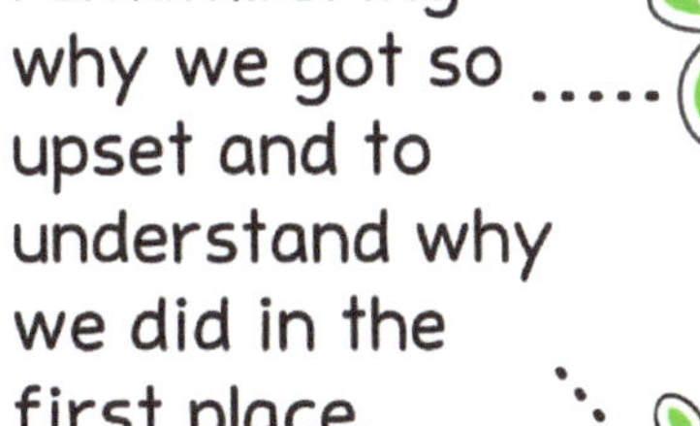

- Representing our memories and programs, what we learn & forget.

- How we, remember, recall, recognize.

- Has a love for elephants because they "never forget."

Help
Initiate
Positive
Programs
Or else!

CAT or a Quoll(QOL)

and the CREATURES of habit

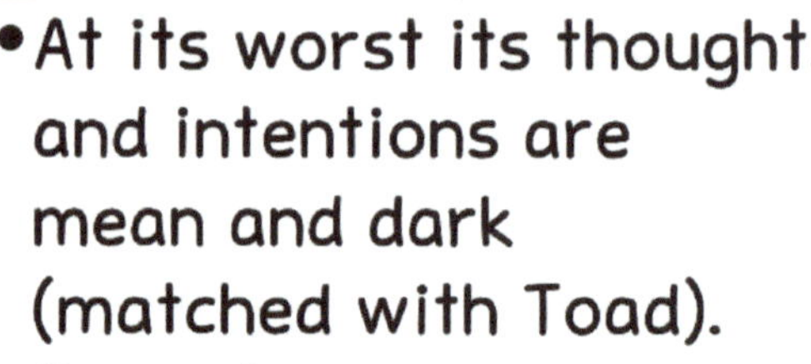

- At its worst its thoughts and intentions are mean and dark (matched with Toad).
- Example: behaviors of feral and abused cats.

Consider Alternatives Thoughtfully

The Glyphs for Cat

Doodles for cat that are simple, easy fun and full of care.

Help you to make a plan that helps everyone involved.

- At its best, it's a Quoll cat focused on maximizing its **Quality of Life.**

Query
Open
Listen

- They are primarily nocturnal.
- The quoll is one of the many unique marsupials found nowhere else except for Australia and New Guinea.
- The quoll is a carnivorous but loves fruit too.

SQUID

and the CREATURES of habit

SQUID
in BRAILLE

- Can you THINK before you INK?

- Why are you poking my SQUID?

The Glyph for Squid

Doodle of the Squid
is just fun and curvy:
how many can you
fit on a page?

How to SQUID!:
Whenever you feel
like something is wrong,
Can you STOP
to ask QUESTIONS
before you move on?
Can you ask good questions
to better UNDERSTAND?
Can you IMAGINE your
choicies, then DECIDE
on a plan?

TOAD (& FROG)

and the CREATURES of habit

TOAD in BRAILLE

EMOTIONS

Name them to Tame them!
You can use a
Wheel of Emotions
to help you
name what
you are feeling.

The Glyphs for Toad

Some doodle
ideas for when
your feelings
are getting
out of hand....
and you just
need a moment.

Tense up body.
Open up body.
Accept?
3**D**'s:
   Defer?
   Deep breathing?
   Distract?

- Represents all
  the croaking
  in our heads of
  our feelings
  and emotions.

- Toads can be
  poisonous!
  Invasive Cane
  Toads in
  Australia
  are deadly
  to cats who
  eat them.

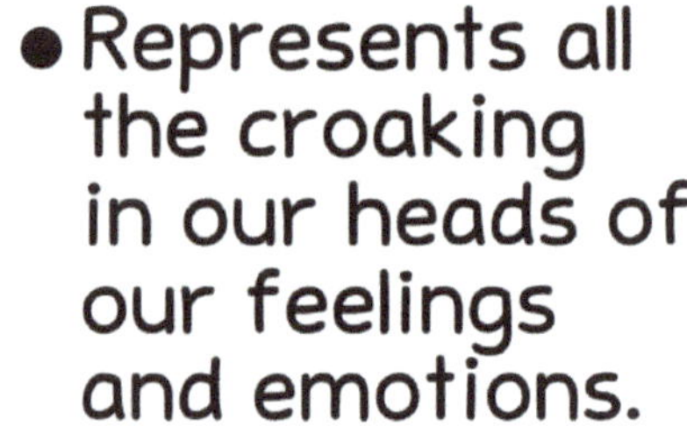

ANTS

and the CREATURES of habit

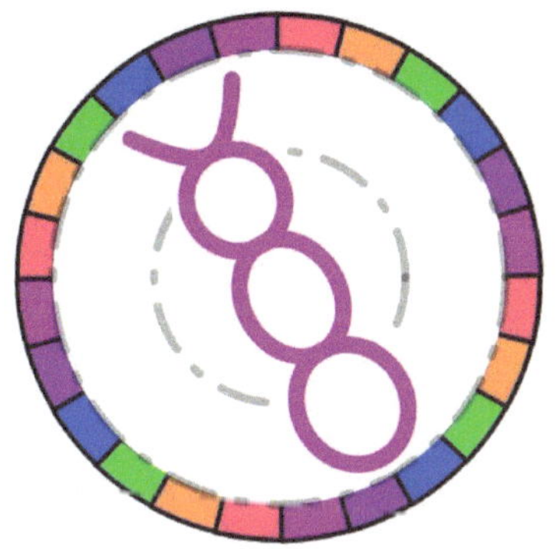

- Representing the neurons at the cellular level, communicating through electron chemicals, passed between the key ingredients for every creature of habit and everything we think,feel and do.

The Glyphs for Ant

Doodles for Ant is super easy. Like a snowman but make the circles all the same size, on one end add two small lines. Make a chain of ants following a path or line. Now your fully distracted! Do you even remember why you were so mad?

- They are the messagers. They are the ones that relay what the other animals are doing. Like sending a text message, instead of a text a creature of habit sends an ant!

Quality of Life eXperiments

Have you ever
  Said or done
  Something you regret?
Have you ever
  Hurt someone
  You cared about?
Have you ever
  Been thoughtless?
  Been careless?
  Been unaware?

We have too.
We're human, too.
  Making choices
  Every day.
  Every moment.

We do not control the moment.
We do not control the situation.

But we can do better.
  Better choices.
  Fewer regrets.

We live in our bubbles
Of "in here" and "out there,"
Of us and of others,
Those far and those near.
We listen to some
And ignore the rest.
Open-minded or not,
Our lives are a test.

How will we survive?
How will we get through our days?
How can we thrive
When we don't know our ways?

Pray, listen to others,
Listen to your voices within.
We can scream. We can cry.
We can laugh. We can grin.
Who are we with others?
Who are we within?

With each new day
We can each try again.

OVERWHELMED

When we feel tension in the throat,
   or tightening in the tummy,
   tears about to flow,
   or any "uh-uh,"
When we begin to feel overwhelmed,
About to drown in an emotional flood,

Our responsive system is telling us,
"Watch out."
Time to SQUID.

If we pinch our finger
   (we don't pinch others),
   gently, just enough
   to distract our emotional brain,
   long enough for us to breathe

And calm,
Get through the moment,
See what is real,

We can regain balance.

Our Quality of
Life (QoL),
is the sum of
the quality
of our moments.

The quality of our
moments depends
on the quality
of our choices.

Better choices
mean fewer
regrets.

SQUID

Your way to
better choices.

Nuestra calidad
de vida
(QOL-Quality of Life)
es la suma
de la Calidad
de nuestros
momentos.

La calidad
de nuestros
momentos
depende
de la calidad
de nuestras
decisiones.

Mejores
decisiones menos
remordimientos.

SQUIDea

tu vida con
mejores
decisiones.

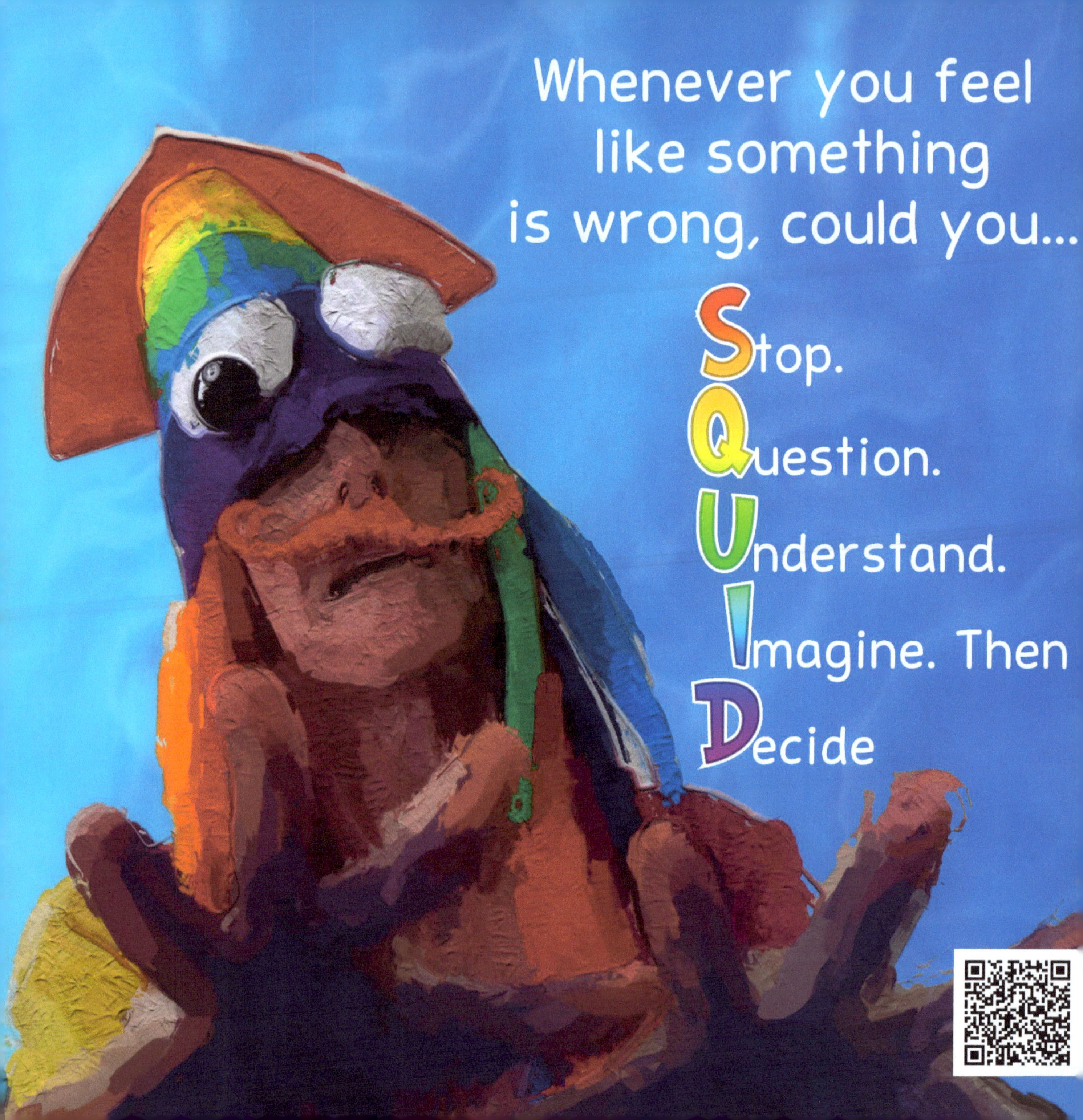

Whenever you feel like something is wrong, could you...
Stop.
Question.
Understand.
Imagine. Then
Decide

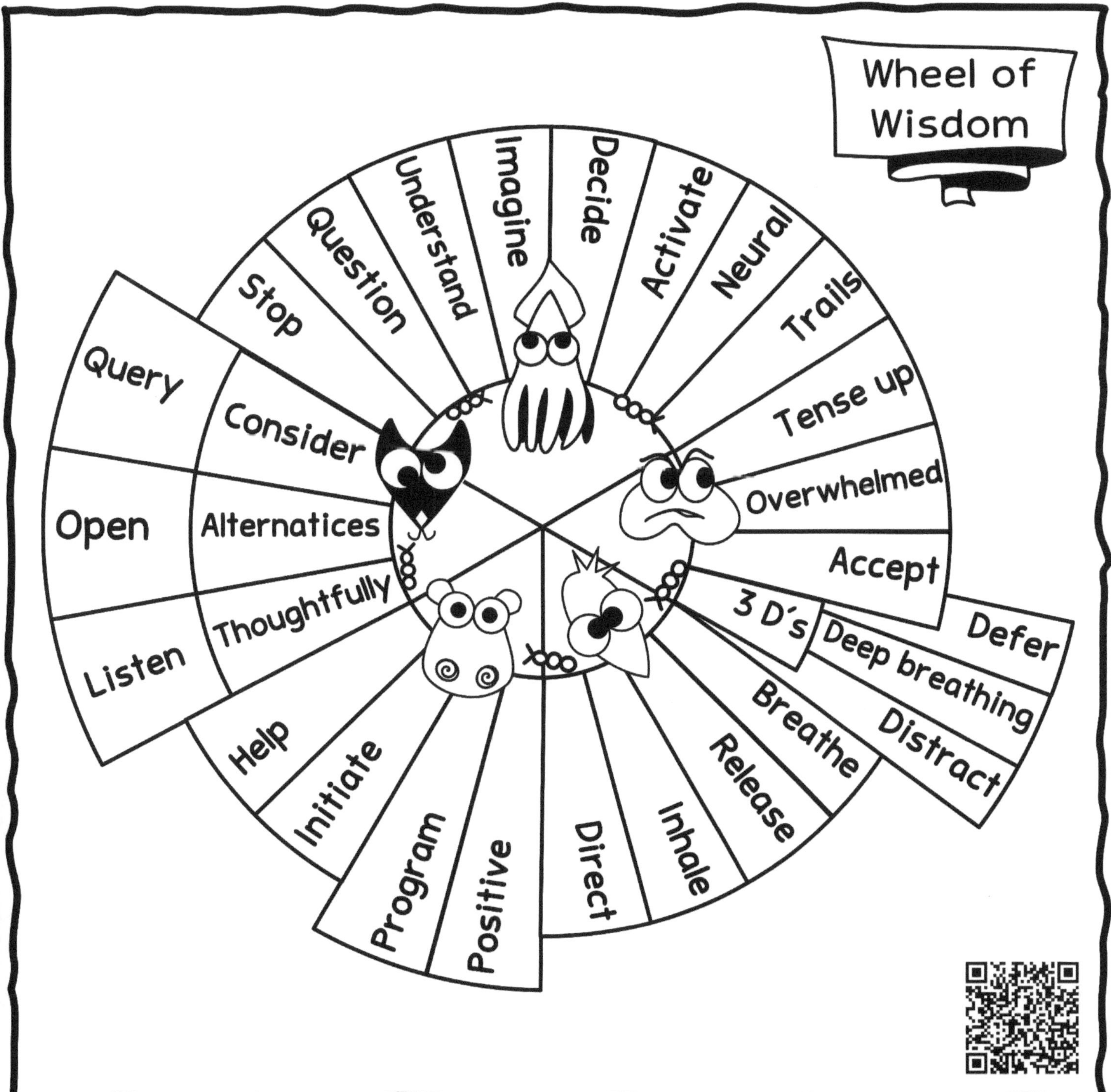

Wheel of Wisdom
Imagine
Understand
Question
Stop
Decide
Activate
Neural
Trails
Query
Consider
Tense up
Open
Alternatices
Overwhelmed
Accept
Listen
Thoughtfully
3 D's
Defer
Deep breathing
Distract
Help
Breathe
Initiate
Release
Program
Inhale
Positive
Direct

So many kind people have helped make these Quality of Life experiments possible – we want to thank you ALL! Thank you for all you do and for being exactly who you are.

And to you who have not yet connected, we enthusiastically invite you to be part of this quality-of-life-changing work! We want to support each of you on your heroic journeys.

Please email squidminders@gmail.com to get links to all the other great stuff we have available to adapt and share wherever you can! Or visit us at www.squidminders.org